ENDORSEMENTS

"This is a responsible, instructional manual in the immediate stabilization and emergency first aid treatment of rescued wildlife."
— Richard A. Alter, D.V.M.

"A reference must for first aid treatment and emergency care for wildlife, for the possible causes of the distress, and the situations under which they occur."
— Mary Hollander, founder
and director, Pesky Critters

"Full of essential, practical information, especially in the area of immediate first aid."
— Laura Simon, president, Connecticut
Wildlife Rehabilitators Association

"This book is for anyone who loves and cares about wildlife. It provides checklists of emergency first aid supplies, checklists of possible problems, checklists of resources, do's and don'ts about when to help, when not, and how."
— Cathy Zamecnik, founder
and director, Little Feet

"This basic handbook will help distressed wildlife in the first emergency stages and answer those first questions about shock and dehydration, diseases, wounds, and fractures, and what to do and who to call."
— Hope M. Douglas, founder
and director, Wind Over Wings

First Aid
For Wildlife

Basic Care For
Birds And Mammals

IRENE RUTH

Illustrated by Hope M. Douglas, M.A.

BICK PUBLISHING HOUSE
MADISON, CT

SECOND EDITION
Fourth Printing
Edited by Richard A. Alter, D.V.M.

Book Design by Jennifer A. Payne
Cover Design by Pearl & Associates

Library of Congress Catalog Card Number: 96-084058

ISBN: 1-884158-14-5--Volume 7
ISBN: 1-884158-04-8--7 Volume Set

Printed by McNaughton & Gunn, Inc.

ACKNOWLEDGMENTS

Our gratitude to the network of Connecticut wildlife rehabilitators that includes Connecticut Wildlife Rehabilitation Association, Wind Over Wings members, and all my own rehabilitator volunteers at Suburban Wildlife, including Pam Dickson of We Rescue, and Karen.

Our special thanks to Dan Mackey, publisher of Wildlife Rehabilitation Magazine Today, and to International Wildlife Rehabilitation Council for their inspiration and standards of excellence.

And our thanks to Laura Simon, president of Connecticut Wildlife Rehabilitation Association; Mary Hollander, director of Pesky Critters; Ron Wulff of Wildlife Sanctuary; Cathy Zamecnik, director of Little Feet.

And thank you, Melissa and Bob.

CONTENTS

INTRODUCTION

This book will not teach you to be a veterinarian. Or a wildlife rehabilitator. What this book will teach you is not to be afraid to help an animal in need of rescue. It will give you basic first aid skills to care for wild birds and mammals until you can get them professional help. The handling skills are those we use currently. Wildlife rehabilitation is a new field. We are learning all the time.

Why should we go out of our way to help an animal in distress? Wouldn't we be interfering with nature? Why we save them may be the wrong question. We save them because they need saving. This is less an interference with nature than we commit every day. Besides, a major percentage of the animals and birds that are received by wildlife rehabilitators to care for are there directly or indirectly because human beings have crowded them out of their habitat or harmed them with their technology. If enough of us "interfere" and help these animals in trouble, maybe we can even up the balance and remind ourselves that without wildlife, human beings cannot long survive.

Remember: These skills are for adult use only. Children should not handle wildlife.

Though helping hurt and distressed animals seems like an easy thing to do, it isn't always as simple as it looks. If helping, raising, and releasing wildlife interests you, you can easily apply for a legal permit. It requires a legal permit to hold and raise wildlife. Please get one. Call your State Department of Environmental Protection (or whatever your state calls its environment

8

conservation department) or your Federal Fish and Wildlife Department for advice, for the telephone number of your nearest local rehabilitator, for information on how you can get training and your own permit.

1

THE RESCUE AND RESCUE KIT

Your reaction to an injured or trapped creature will be almost instinctive; you will want to relieve the animal of its distress immediately. But think before you act. Use your head before you let your heart reaction kick in. You need to assess the situation and then decide whether you will—or can—assist this animal.

EVALUATION

Each situation will be different and must be evaluated. Ask these questions.

- What kind of animal is this?
- Is it an adult or a juvenile?
- What is its situation?
- Does it actually need your help?
- Is it possible for you to help it?
- Is it safe for you to help it?

A few minutes now can save both you and the animal trouble later on. Animals have defenses. Remember these, and treat their defenses with respect and understanding. They aren't much against our guns.

a) Safety for the Animal
- Do not critternap—a fledgling may only be learning to fly; fawn and rabbit babies are often left alone for hours while mothers feed

- Watch and wait at least 4 hours for rabbits and fawns; at least 2 hours for raccoon mothers to return: call a rehabilitator for advice

b) Safety for You
- Never handle a bird too large to manage easily
- Watch for beaks and claws; do not handle raptors such as hawks and eagles by yourself (call for professional help)
- Rabies species, including raccoons, skunks, foxes, bats, **are not** necessarily sick if out in daytime and may just be hungry: to determine illness, watch for central nervous system symptoms (convulsions, facial spasms, paralysis, staggering) and remember that these may also be due to a car hit or distemper

GUIDELINES

Here are a few guidelines to help you decide if an animal needs to be rescued.

Help a bird if:
- There is blood, an open wound, or a recognizable break
- It cannot stand on its own
- One of its legs is hanging useless
- It cannot fly and is not a nestling or fledgling being coached by nearby parents (always watch and wait to make certain it is orphaned)

- The beak is damaged
- It has oil on its feathers
- It is definitely caught in a trap
- You recognize it as an exotic species (these cannot fend for themselves)
- It is a bird of prey or swan having only one foot or leg, or there is a fishing line or string caught on the bird
- The bird has been caught by a cat even if it seems fine
- The bird is unconscious
- If there is any difficulty breathing

Leave the bird alone if:
- You are not absolutely certain it is orphaned
- It is a swan grazing in a field
- It is standing on one leg
- It is any bird with only one eye except hawks
- You would endanger yourself and others

Help a mammal if:
- You can see open wounds or other injuries
- It has been hit by a car
- A leg appears damaged
- It is dragging two legs
- It is caught in a fence or trap
- It has been attacked by a predator
- It has been caught by a cat, even if it seems fine
- It is an orphan not ready to be on its own (you wait and watch to see if the mother is simply away foraging for food, or the nest is destroyed and the

Animals love their young

mother waiting until you leave to move her babies)
- The animal is unconscious
- It is having trouble breathing

Leave a mammal alone if:
- It is a normally nocturnal animal out during the day (it may be just hungry or a nursing mother looking for extra food)
- You are not absolutely certain an infant or juvenile is an orphan
- The animal is too big or too dangerous for you to handle safely (any hurt animal may bite or become aggressive), call your Department of Environmental Protection or U.S. Fish and Wildlife Department, or the local police—have numbers handy
- It is showing possible signs of rabies (lack of coordination, circling, unprovoked aggressiveness,

drooling, convulsing, facial tics, paralysis, or
extreme tameness): if these signs are present, notify
the police or animal control officer, and do not
touch the animal or allow other humans and animals
to approach

IMMEDIATE AID

If you have decided that the animal needs your care, be calm
and deliberate. A deep breath helps. You will make fewer mis-
takes, and the animal will react positively to your calm.

First make sure that you have everything you are going to
need. You can't put a rescue on hold while you go get something
you have forgotten. Carry some simple items in your car and
your work can begin right away.

ITEMS FOR YOUR CAR

- a strong, covered, ventilated container, heavy cardboard
  or plastic (this protects you and comforts and contains the
  animal)

- blanket, towels

- thick gloves for your protection

- a lightweight shovel (often better than hands for lifting an
  injured animal into container or to the side of the road—an
  injured creature may bite or carry parasites)

- wire cutters and scissors for traps, fences, fishing line, and
  so forth

THE CAPTURE

Be calm, and move quietly and smoothly. Make all of your actions firm but gentle. Quiet talk seems to reassure some animals, but watch for reactions and stop if it seems to upset.

Avoid looking directly into an animal's eyes, as a direct gaze is sometimes seen as threatening. Remember we are a predator species; they are right to fear us.

Your own protection should be your top priority. If you are injured helping this animal, who will be available to help the others?

Wear gloves, heavy ones like welding gloves, for picking up mammals and the large birds, rubber gloves for smaller birds and infants. Keep your face out of the animal's reach and protect your eyes.

Don't put yourself in danger by climbing high trees, going near powerlines, trying to work in pitch dark, going into traffic.

You will have better luck with your capture if you guide or lure rather than chase an animal into confinement. Herding into a corner situation such as a building, fence, or wall will give you an advantage during capture, but keep in mind that the animal is now cornered, will feel threatened, and may attack.

Approach with caution, but be purposeful. Anticipate a struggle. A humane trap for an adult animal or a possibly rabid one is the best and safest rescue. Keep physical contact to a minimum for your safety and the animal's well-being. Trap and transport. Wear heavy gloves when handling trap. Cover the small bird or mammal with a blanket or towel, your own coat. If it can't see, it will be less apt to struggle. Bring the blanket under and around the animal, trapping wings against the body on birds, and keeping paws and claws covered in mammals.

Put into the transport box and secure immediately. Be as quiet as possible during the capture.

Use only as much restraint as needed, but never underestimate your patient. A terrified animal is stronger than usual.

All creatures have a fight or flight response to danger. Be ready for either.

SITUATIONS

The following are situations in which an animal may be injured or need help.

1. **Car Hits.** Animals that are slow are often hit by cars and trucks. Squirrels are fast, but are hit often because they can't seem to make up their minds which way is safe to go. Crows and hawks are often hit eating roadkill, and owls are hit while chasing small mammals. If you can, without endangering your own life, stop to rescue a wounded animal. If you can, stop to shovel-carry a roadkill to the side of the road, and you will save the life of a hungry animal.

2. **Traps and Snares.** Leg hold traps cause terrible damage to a bird or mammal. Even humane traps like the Havahart traps can be dangerous to an animal who panics and tries to fight its way out or one who has been left in the trap too long without food or water. A bird or mammal may be trapped in a house or office building, a chimney, drainage pipes, barrels, fences, barbed wire, fishing line, garden or sports netting. They may need help because of dehydration or

starvation, because of injuries from whatever they were trapped in, or because of injuries sustained while trying to escape. There are animals who will chew at their own legs to escape.

3. **Gunshot Wounds.** Hunters, and people "defending" their property against wildlife can wound an animal. Sometimes animals are shot in acts of cruelty and abuse. The animal may escape, but eventually the wound, loss of blood, infection, or stress will take its toll and the animal will need help.

4. **Predator Attack**. All wildlife has natural predators and may sustain tooth and claw injuries from other animals. Humans are predators too, and can intentionally or accidentally cause injuries to wild animals.

5. **Window Hits.** Birds are often injured by flying into windows. They see scenery reflections, not glass.

6. **Glass, Wire, Sharp Metal, Sharp Sticks, Rocks** are all a threat to wild animals.

7. **Fires** in woods or forest areas.

8. **Falls and Slips.** Just living its own life, an animal can be prey to falls and slips from trees, cliffs, slippery rocks, into pools, lakes, ponds, rivers.

9. **Food or Water Shortage.** A bad winter takes its toll, a drought.

10.   **Extreme Weather Conditions.**

11.   **Oil Spills, Tar, Chemicals** used in swimming pools, on lawns, in cars.

12.   **Careless Litter** such as the uncut holes of six-pack plastic, balloons, and fishing lines that can choke, be swallowed, or tangle legs and beaks to cause drowning or starvation.

13.   **Lawn Mowers** run over nests of rabbits, moles, shrews, and other small ones.

14.   **Diseases and Parasites.**

Try to find out as much as possible about the situation that caused an emergency for the animal. This information can be an important tool in your rescue, in the first aid treatment, and for the professional.

Just a duck

2

HOME AND FIRST AID SUPPLIES

You now have the animal secured in its box, away from out-side dangers, and you are ready to begin to help. The ideal situation is to get the animal to a veterinarian who works with wild animals, or to a wildlife rehabilitator who has experience working with orphaned or injured wildlife. Check with veteri-narians in your area to see if they are willing to help. Call your local wildlife department to find the names and telephone num-bers of rehabilitators near you. Keep these numbers available.

If you can reach someone to help you right away, your work is done. Unfortunately, it is not always possible to reach some-one right away. In the meantime, you will want to make the crit-ter as comfortable as possible. You may not be able to fix the injuries or cure the illnesses, but you can stabilize the animals and keep them alive until you can get some professional help.

HOME FIRST AID KIT

These items compose a useful home first aid kit for emer-gency situations.

- a suitable cage or container, cardboard box, plastic box (make sure there are air holes)

- Betadine, Clinidine, Nolvasan, or similar antiseptic wash (do not use hydrogen peroxide as it spreads bacteria into healthy tissue)

- triple antibiotic ointment, germicidal soap, petroleum jelly

- a dehydrating solution such as Pedialyte (any supermarket in baby section), Lactated Ringers (veterinarian supply), or you can make your own with:

1 quart warm water	1 cup warm water
3 Tablespoons sugar	3/4 Tablespoon sugar
1 teaspoon salt	1/4 teaspoon salt

- Kaopectate or Pepto Bismol
- flea and tick water-based (safe for kittens) liquid spray containing pyrethrins (powders can be inhaled and damage eyes of birds and small mammals)
- syringes, eyedropper
- tweezers
- bandages, gauze and cotton, and tape, adhesive, masking or nonstick
- towels, soft cloths, blankets (no ragged edges, loops, holes)
- paper towels
- rubber gloves
- heavy, protective gloves, like fireplace or welders gloves
- can of puppy or kitten milk replacer, applesauce, baby rice cereal

3

PROBLEM CHECKLIST AND THE PHYSICAL EXAMINATION

PROBLEM CHECKLIST

There is a moment of fear when you first hold a distressed creature. You do not know what is wrong. You are not certain you can deal with the injury or illness. You doubt your knowledge and capacities. It will help to go over this general checklist in your mind, to answer your own questions and those of the professional you call and to whom you will take this animal.

Major Categories of Problems in Distressed Animals

  I.   Shock

  II.   Dehydration

  III. Unconsciousness

  IV.   Wounds (injuries involving breaks in the skin)

  V.   Fractures
        A. Simple—no bones protruding
        B. Compound—bone ends protruding through skin

  VI.   Poisoning

  VII. Malnutrition and Starvation

22

VIII. Diseases and Infections
    A. Virus
    B. Bacteria
    C. Parasites, external, internal
    D. Zoonotic—diseases that affect humans

IX. Burns and Scalds

X. Hypothermia and Hyperthermia

Systems That Can Be Affected

Respiratory	Skeletal	Skin
Nervous	Digestive	Eye and Ear
Muscular		Blood

Some Causes of Problems

- Inherited or Birth Condition
- Transmitted (from another animal)
- Accidents
- Abuse
- Predator Attack
- Parasites
- Infection
- Runtiness

Think about possible causes, symptoms, and then the appropriate treatment.

THE PHYSICAL EXAM

Preparation

Treat any animal you work with for shock. Once you get it home, place it in a container in a warm, dark, quiet place. Cover the cage or box to reduce visual stress. This is a time for the animal to rest and recover a bit from the stress of the capture and transportation. It is also a time for you to be doing the first part of your physical exam of the mammal or bird...observe. Learn as much as you can before you even begin the hands on part of the exam. This includes watching the animal and referring to your books, both the general reference guides on the creature in its natural habitat so you understand its normal conditions, and any manuals you have on rehabilitation.

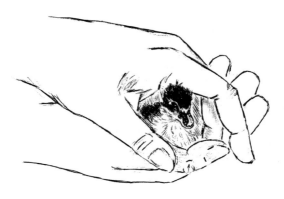

Holding and warming a small one

While the animal rests and you observe, get your supplies ready. Have at hand anything you might possibly need during the exam.

Prepare a gentle surface for the animal to rest on during the exam: toweling, layers of soft cloth, an old sweatshirt.

Have extra soft cloths, bandages, and an antiseptic solution like Betadine ready.

Be prepared for maggots (these look like tiny white worms and are usually very active) in any wound. Remember that these can be a helpful cleansing agent, but do not leave them. You will need to rinse repeatedly with saline solution or other antiseptic rinse, which will cause them to begin to move out of the wound. Use tweezers to remove any that do not rinse out.

Have a plan for examination that you follow consistently with every animal or bird. Start the exam with the head, not forgetting the mouth, and work toward the tail. Or do it in the reverse. The order does not matter, but be consistent and there will be less chance of forgetting something during the actual exam. If you find something wrong, don't stop there. It might not be the only problem. Check everything. A bird with an obvious broken leg may also be choking on an object in its throat.

Wash your hands before and after handling any animal. Wear gloves.

Remember: any injured juvenile or adult can add teeth and agility to its fear of you. It will try to escape. It may claw or bite. It will not enjoy the exam. Be prepared.

While you are doing the exam, look for any signs of ticks and fleas.

Some stress is inevitable during an exam. But if at any time during the exam the animal becomes too stressed (begins to breathe too heavily, struggles enough to hurt itself or you, screams in terror or pain) stop the exam and allow the creature dark and quiet, and then begin again. Too much stress can kill an animal.

Always be on the alert for wounds, punctures, cuts. If you find any, be sure to check for maggots, or maggot eggs, which are beige and look like flakes of oatmeal.

THE EXAMINATION

Head

Are there wounds? Are the eyes bright or sunken? Are they runny? Swollen? Crusty? Closed or opened? Do they respond to light or touch? Are there any maggots, or other foreign objects? A rapid vibration of the eyes may be an indication of concussion.

Check inside the mouth, being very careful. Note the color of the gums. Pale or white gums can mean internal bleeding or anemia. Are the teeth all right? Is there foreign matter like dirt in the mouth? Is there an object in the throat? Is there bleeding from the mouth? Is there beak or jaw damage?

Are the ears clean? Is there bleeding? Are there mites, ticks? Is there a discharge?

Is the neck all right? Does the head wobble? (If the creature is a baby bird, this is normal. Otherwise, it isn't.) Is there head twitch or tilt? Are there wounds?

Limbs

Are there breaks or fractures? Sometimes these are obvious, sometimes you need to compare the right and left limbs to see if there is an abnormality in one by feeling gently along the limbs and into shoulder and hip. Are there breaks in the skin, swelling, misalignments? Are the feet all right?

Body

Are the feathers or fur in good condition? Are they dull, scruffy? Do you see oil or other substances on them?

Feel the chest and abdomen areas, checking for wounds. A sharp, thin keel in birds indicates starvation.

Check the behind to see if there are signs of diarrhea, constipation, prolapsed rectum, worms.

Skin should be loose and pliable, and in mammals provides a good test for dehydration. It should flatten in less than two seconds if pinched into a tent. If the skin is slow to flatten, dehydration is present. The best place to pinch is between the shoulders. For a bird, pinching skin to test for dehydration is unreliable. In birds, dehydration is signaled by apathy, sharp keel (the bird is too thin), slitted and sunken eyes, and a hunched look of misery.

Are there any odors besides the animal's natural odor? Many people, even without training, can detect a sickish odor on an animal in trouble as they can on their own children. Wounds that are infected have a strong odor.

Weigh the animal if it is possible to do so.

Make notes during the examination if you have some help, after the exam if you are working alone. Write down anything you noted during the exam. All of this information will help the veterinarian or rehabilitator later on. Record the critter's weight if you can. This will be important in deciding dosages of medications.

Now make the animal comfortable, and begin to deal with the conditions that you have found.

4

EMERGENCY SITUATIONS AND TREATMENT

No treatment should begin on an animal until the animal has been treated for shock by warming, and kept in a dark, quiet place for at least half an hour. You will know if it is warm enough if it feels warm to the touch.

1. Shock

Symptoms: Drop in body temperature, body feels cold to the touch, a fast but weak pulse, fast, shallow breathing. Lips, gums, tongue, and eye membranes may be pale (this could also indicate internal bleeding). There may also be vomiting, loss of control of urine and bowels, general weakness, and perhaps unconsciousness. Shock reactions in birds can be delayed, sometimes as long as a couple of days. The bird will be weak, listless, have pale membranes.

Causes: Extreme stress, physical or emotional.

Treatment: Keep the shocked animal in a dark, warm, quiet place. Cover the cage or container to reduce visual stress. The animal should have some time of complete isolation.

2. Dehydration or Excessive Loss of Fluids

Symptoms: Sunken eyes, overall shrunken appearance, loss of skin elasticity, non-responsiveness.

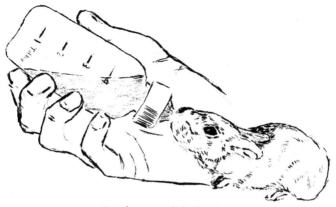

Feed mammals belly down

Causes: Extreme heat, no available water, prolonged or severe diarrhea.

Treatment: Treat by restoring body fluids. Use Pedialyte, Lactated Ringers solution, or a homemade rehydration solution (1 quart of warm water, 3 Tablespoons of sugar, and one teaspoon of salt, mixed well) to balance the animal's electrolytes. Give this solution by mouth several times within the first hour. For a small mammal, you can use a pet nurser with a nipple, a syringe with a nipple, eye dropper. For larger mammals, an ordinary baby's bottle will do or a large syringe. For birds, the fluid must be dropped onto the beak and allowed to dribble into the mouth. **Do not put fluids directly into a bird's mouth**, or you risk drowning it by getting fluids into its breathing hole. Alternately, feed small bits of watermelon, berries, or grapes instead of the fluids. When the animal or bird seems more alert and responsive, other food may be introduced slowly.

A severely dehydrated animal will need intravenous fluids or subcutaneous fluid injections or drips. This must be done by a qualified professional.

3. Unconsciousness

Symptoms: Little or no response to stimuli.

Causes: Concussion, hypothermia, heat stroke, suffocation, drowning, heart attack, electrocution, and shock can all cause various degrees of unconsciousness.

Treatment: Concussion or stunning is usually caused by a blow to the head, and is temporary. The animal will recover on its own if treated as for shock with a safe, warm, quiet, dark place to rest.

A more serious injury will make the animal unconscious longer. The animal may have trouble with balance or paralysis, and possibly blindness. The animal needs to be checked out by a veterinarian, and possibly treated with steroids to lessen damage from tissue swelling.

Coma is deep unconsciousness, and there will be no reflexes evident at all. This can result from severe brain injury, poisoning, or high temperatures. This condition also needs veterinary care.

4. Open Wounds and Bleeding

Symptoms: Blood, visible tears in the flesh.

Causes and Types:

a. incisions—caused by sharp, tearing objects like glass or metal

b. punctures and closed wounds—caused by sharp, pointy objects like nails, teeth, sharp sticks, thorns, and by bullets or pellets (especially dangerous as the flesh may seal over them and they can become infected easily; punctures may also be much deeper than they appear)

c. lacerations—torn flesh usually with jagged edges (these require veterinary attention)

d. bruises and scrapes can be caused by skidding on a hard surface, by kicks or blows from a stick or club—there may not be much bleeding involved superficially

Treatment: To stop severe bleeding, apply pressure. If the blood spurts, it is from an artery, and pressure with gauze should be applied from above the wound for at least 5 to 10 minutes. If the blood flows, it is from a vein, and pressure should be applied from below for at least 2 minutes. Do not check to see if bleeding has stopped until time has elapsed. Repeat if necessary. Do not dab, or you will disturb the clot.

A wound must be cleaned carefully with warm water. Wet a soft cloth or gauze pad and clean the wound gently from the center of the wound out to the edges. The animal won't like this, but it is an important part of the treatment. Take your time. To be sure any fur, dirt, and feathers stay out of the wound, smear petroleum jelly around, not in, the wound area. The fur or feathers will stick together instead of falling into the wound.

Check carefully for signs of maggots and maggot eggs. Check for overlooked particles and use tweezers or gauze to remove gently.

Once the wound is absolutely clean, dry gently and apply antibiotic cream (or rinse, if the wound is deeper, with Betadine or other antiseptic or antibiotic solution). Hydrogen peroxide is not desirable because of the foaming action. Cover with a clean bandage or a clean, nonstick gauze pad, wrapping this with vet wrap to secure the pad. You may have to secure with tape, but use as little as possible. Do not wrap too tightly or you will constrict breathing or blood supply, particularly with birds.

Once a day, more often if needed, remove the dressing, reclean the wound, and reapply a fresh dressing.

5. Infected Wounds and Abscesses

Symptoms and Causes: An existing wound may be contaminated, and become swollen and red. There will be white, yellow, or green pus and fluids in the wound. An abscess is a wound that has closed superficially, lacks air enough to heal, and contains the pus and fluids below the surface. The skin may be swollen and red, will usually feel warm to the touch. An infected wound may smell bad. It may contain maggots.

Treatment: Clean out any maggots or debris. A maggot is the larva of an insect such as a fly. The fly is attracted to an open wound and lays its eggs; within hours, the eggs have hatched to tiny maggots. They do serve a useful purpose by keeping the wound clean and free of infection when they eat dead flesh. They multiply rapidly though, and will eventually penetrate to a vital organ and kill the animal.

To remove maggots from eyes, use sterilized water such

32

as contact lens saline solution. Use an eyedropper to drop the water into the eye, and then suck it back up again. Large maggots will be stuck to the end of the dropper, small ones will be sucked in. Dispose of them and repeat the process.

For maggots on body wounds, flush with saline solution repeatedly. Sometimes a heavy coat of cornstarch will work for a superficial wound. The maggots need a wet area to move freely. When the cornstarch dries, they'll drop off. Then wash off the rest of the cornstarch and treat the wound. Maggot eggs are yellow, look somewhat like flakes of corn meal, and appear in groups or clumps which are sometimes very large. If the maggot eggs haven't hatched yet, tissue or gauze with petroleum jelly, mineral oil, or olive oil on it will help to remove them. A flea comb will help to get them out of fur. Wash the area well before continuing to treat the wound.

Examine the animal several times a day until you are sure all of the maggots are gone. When the wound is free of maggots and debris, coat the fur or feathers around the wound with petroleum jelly, and then clip. This will help to keep the wound clean. Apply hot packs soaked in a solution of 1 pint of hot water with two teaspoons of salt. Keep the pack on the wound 10 minutes at a time and repeat every 2 hours. In the case of an abscess, continue until the abscess opens and drains.

An antibiotic cream can be found in the drug or grocery store (any generic triple antibiotic cream will serve the purpose), and should be applied to the wound. Oral antibiotics such as Amoxicillin, Baytril, or Clavamox should be prescribed by a veterinarian according to the type and weight of the animal.

6. Fractures

Symptoms: There may be obvious deformity or swelling, an inability to use the affected part. Fractures or broken bones require emergency veterinary care. The animal may also be in shock, and may be bleeding. *Do not try to fix without a veterinarian.*

Causes: Car hits, falls, traps, twisting or slipping, gunshots, impact with windows, wires, cruelty.

Treatment: All breaks and fractures should be treated by a veterinarian quickly, but you should stabilize the animal by treating for shock.

A simple fracture has no bone ends protruding. A compound fracture has bone ends protruding through the skin.

Do not try to set or splint a fracture yourself. You will cause more pain than relief and will probably make the fracture worse. If the fracture is compound, control any bleeding. Try not to let anything touch the bone to protect against infection. If possible (the animal may fight you) apply a sterile bandage or gauze pad and wrap lightly where the bones are protruding. Put the animal in a small box so that there is not much room for it to move around. A strong cardboard box or plastic storage bin with holes in the lid for air is a safe container to use. Wire cages or dog carriers may cause further damage to the broken limb. Transport the animal in this container to a veterinarian or rehabilitator.

7. Poisoning

Symptoms, Causes, and Treatments: There are many different ways that a mammal or bird can be poisoned. The

Treatment: Give the animal rehydration fluid using the methods described under Dehydration on page 23. If you must keep the animal overnight before getting it to a rehabilitator, feed it small amounts of easily digestible foods such as commercial human liquid diet or prescription dog or cat canned food products for convalescing cats and dogs, which can be gotten from your veterinarian. For birds, you will need to consult a rehabilitator for the proper species-specific diet. You can always begin with bits of peeled grape, watermelon, moistened kibble, moist canned dog or cat food, finger-feeding if necessary.

NOTE: Sometimes starvation is caused by digestive development problems, disease, parasites, or a mechanical cause such a something caught in the throat or a poison. Get advice and help.

9. External and Internal Parasites

Symptoms and Treatment of External Parasites: These can be seen in the fur or feathers of the animal. Feather mites are often difficult to spot on a bird, but if you hold the bird, the warmth of your skin will cause them to travel to your hand where they can be seen and felt.

External parasites can weaken a compromised animal. Dampen a cloth or paper towel with liquid insecticide such as ParaMist. Pat this over the animal, being careful of the eyes. Start at the neck so that the parasites don't travel to the head. Pull out ticks with tweezers.

Symptoms and Treatment of Internal Parasites: A great number of animals are carrying internal parasites. They may not be the main problem of the bird or mammal that are dealing with but may make recovery slower. A fecal sample may be examined at a veterinary office, and indicate the presence of parasites or bacteria that can be treated with prescription medicines. Your veterinarian will help you with the type of medications and dosages if you are a licensed wildlife rehabilitator.

10. Diseases

Symptoms: Some of these include: apathy, lack of appetite, seizures, paralysis, circling motions, screeching, lack of coordination, runny eyes and nose, diarrhea, and feathers or fur in poor shape. Fever, and a sickly odor, may also indicate a disease.

Treatment: Disease requires a veterinarian. Bring stool samples and all of the information that you have collected about the animal.

Zoonoses: These are diseases wildlife transmits to humans. Rabies (see p. 7), tetanus, psittacosis (from pigeons), and salmonellosis are among them. Baylisascaris procynosis is a roundworm problem found in raccoon feces that can cause severe central nervous system trouble.

If you suspect an animal is diseased, protect yourself and all other animals. Isolate the sick animal and get it promptly to a vet. Wear gloves, wash hands with antibacterial disinfectant soap, and use a disinfectant to wash anything the animal had contact with, especially surfaces contaminated with feces, urine, saliva.

11. Fever

Fever is a symptom of disease, parasites, infections, and other problems. Although the fever itself can be treated, the cause of the fever must be found and treated.

12. Burns and Scalds

Symptoms: Singed feathers or fur, reddening of skin, tissue damage.

Causes: Burns and scalds are caused by direct contact with flames or a hot surface, flying cinders, steam, sparks, hot fluids, cooking oil, hot tar, and caustic chemicals, lightning, live electrical wires.

Treatment: Clean the area with a sterile salt solution or contact lens solution. Apply ice packs or immerse the area in cold water to cool the flesh and help relieve the pain. Put petroleum jelly around the burn and clip the fur or feathers in the area. The jelly will keep fur or feathers from falling onto the injured area. **Never use butter, oil, or oil-based ointment on the burn.** Apply a cream antibiotic on the site and cover with a nonstick bandage.

13. Hyperthermia or Heatstroke

Symptoms: Obvious distress, panting, lethargy; animal may have trouble walking, and may stagger and fall if it tries to move. The body temperature will be very high, and there may be convulsions or loss of consciousness.

Causes: Hot environment.

Treatment: Get animal to a cool place, and reduce its body heat. Use cold water, gently poured over the animal, cool cloths or ice packs, get paws or feet into cool water. Keep this up until the animal comes around.

14. Hypothermia or Extreme Cooling of Body Temperature

Symptoms: The body temperature will be very low, the pulse will be weak, and slow. Breathing will be slow and shallow. Skin may feel cool to the touch.

Causes: Cold weather, cold environment.

Treatment: Get animal to a warm place, and begin to warm gradually. Cover with blankets (if small, cup in hands, warm against body). Then place in container or cage. Provide a heat source, such as a heating pad set to low put under 1/3 of the cage or container the animal rests in. A 60 watt light bulb 12" to 18" over a container can provide a steady heat.

If frostbite is involved, extremities will become numb. The affected areas may become pale and then turn red and scaly. A bird's feet will be red and swollen. Don't plunge the areas into hot water or rub them. Warm gradually.

15. Diarrhea

Symptoms: Loose or watery stool, sometimes with blood or mucus.

Causes: A bacterial infection, internal parasites, viral infections, overeating or changes in the diet (expect some at first because we will not be able to reproduce natural diet), nervousness or stress, reactions to poisons or heavy metal ingestion, allergy to food or drugs.

Treatment: Pepto Bismol or Kaopectate, doses adjusted to weight of animal. If the diarrhea continues, or has blood in it, check with a vet. You will need a fecal sample done to check for internal parasites, or the vet may recommend an antibacterial, antifungal, or a worming medication.

16. Bloat (or Constipation)

Symptoms: Mammal's belly is tight with skin stretched almost to transparency. After feeding, the belly should feel like a marshmallow, not a hard rubber ball.

Causes: Internal parasites, a change in diet, improper diet, overfeeding, or constipation. Also there may be an internal malfunction, as in runtiness (see p. 37).

Treatment: Gas or fecal matter causing the bloat must be expelled. Lay the mammal belly down on a heating pad on low setting or hold a small creature in your hand under warm running water or in a cup bath. Gently but firmly massage from rib cage toward tail. Powdered activated charcoal or powdered calcium carbonate dissolved in water, or small amount of anti-gas medication such as simethicone may help. Infant gas relief drops are appropriate.

17. Eyes, Ears, and Noses

Foreign bodies in eyes may sometimes be removed with a saline wash. If you have no commercial saline solution for eyes, make your own by completely dissolving a teaspoon of salt in a pint of warm water. Saline can also be used to unstick eyelids that have become stuck together. A warm, wet cloth held gently to the eye will also help.

If an animal rubs or shakes its head, or holds its head tilted to one side, paws or scratches the ear, there may be a foreign object in the ear, or there may be earmites present. If the ear seems dirty, clean some of the dirt out and place it on a damp paper towel. If the towel turns red, there are mites present.

There may be dirt in the mouth and nose of an orphaned baby who has been on the ground. Be sure to clean this out before trying to rehydrate or feed.

18. Runtiness

Symptoms: Low body weight, slow behavioral and physical development, lack of muscle mass, possible sickly and pale appearance—or there may be what seems normal development that suddenly slows or stops. There may be regression.

There are two types of runtiness. In Type 1, the animal shows a behavioral and physical development about one to three weeks behind the normal stages for its age group but is otherwise healthy. These babies are sometimes referred to as late bloomers. In Type 2, the animals will never develop properly. There are abnormalities in the blood, respiratory, and digestive systems based on permanently underdeveloped systems. These babies exhibit loose stools, intestinal gas (bloat), fluid build-up in the abdomen, irregular heart rates, and are pale, sickly, and inactive. Fur is dull, smell is not normal, eyes may not be alert. Long past schedule, these babies continue to urinate on each other, foul the nest and themselves. Weight and development remain retarded. These babies seldom live long; death may be sudden.

Causes: Immature mother, lack of maternal nutrition, unknown causes.

Treatment: Add Nutrical to diet, warmth, watchfulness.

OTHER EMERGENCIES

19. Cat-Caught Animal

Symptoms: Tears in the flesh, punctures (not always visible), crushing injuries in small birds and mammals. Often the victim will appear fine, but don't be fooled. Cat saliva received through an open wound or puncture has potent bacteria that can kill a small creature in 72 hours.

Treatment: Treat for shock. Once the animal is calm, clean the visible wounds and double check carefully to make sure you have found all injuries. Apply topical antibiotics. A veterinarian should administer internal antibiotics as soon as possible and oral antibiotics to continue the treatment for three to five days. Rabbits and deer react badly to oral antibiotics and will need them administered by injection.

infant less than
one hour old

mallard juvenile
Ages & Stages of Ducks

20. Air Bubbles

Symptoms: An air bubble may appear under the skin of injured birds. Don't mistake a full crop (on the side of the neck) in some birds for an air bubble. There will be no food visible through the skin of an air bubble.

Causes: An injury will sometimes result in an air leak under the skin.

Treatment: It may deflate on its own. If it does not, and if it is causing pressure or getting in the way of normal movement, have a veterinarian puncture it with a sterile needle, express the air out, and seal the hole with an antibiotic ointment. It may recur within an hour or so, and the procedure must be repeated.

21. Oiled Birds

Symptoms: Oil can be seen on feathers, waterproofing and insulating properties will be gone, bird may be chilled, unable to fly. Waterbirds will not be able to remain afloat.

Causes: Oil spills from shore or tankers on the water.

Treatment: Keep the bird warm through the treatment. Wash out the eyes, mouth, and nostrils. Use Dawn dishwashing liquid in a 5% Dawn to 95% warm water solution. Gently pour the solution over the feathers while stroking in the direction of growth. Do not scrub. Rinse with lots of warm water. Be careful of the eye area. Keep rinsing until water rolls off of the bird in droplets.

Get the bird to a wildlife rehabilitator. Getting an oiled bird ready for release is complicated and may take weeks of specialized care.

ABUSE AND CRUELTY

Sadly, ours is a species that uses other species for sport and for transferring our own rage. Rehabilitators and veterinarians often receive wildlife that has been stoned, shot at, run over for fun by motorboats, pickup trucks, cars. Animals that are beaten, starved, and generally maltreated must receive care as well as those shot at, downed, but not killed. Please be aware. Please rescue.

5
HANDLING AND RELEASE

Whether the only problem your animal has is being an orphan, or you are temporarily feeding and housing a wounded baby or adult, you will need to know something about captive diet, captive housing, and general handling and release techniques.

INITIAL ORPHAN CARE

If the only problem is that this is an orphan baby, otherwise healthy, then put it in a container and keep it warm.

Most babies cannot regulate their own temperatures and need help from a heating pad on low under 1/3 of the container (not inside the container, and only under part of the container so the

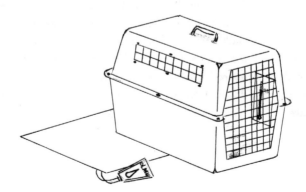

Pet carrier, heating pad on low, thermometer

baby can crawl away from the heat if it wants to). A 60 watt light bulb may be used 12" to 18" above half of the box. Whatever source you use, be sure to check the temperature often. A thermometer is a wise investment.

Mammals

A mammal baby will need to be fed a formula as close as possible to its mother's milk. The size of the infant will determine what kind of feeding instrument to use. You may choose an eyedropper, syringe, kitten-sized feeder bottle, or a regular baby bottle. The baby's first meals will be Pedialyte or other rehydrating fluid. Assume that if it is away from mom, it is dehydrated. The fluid is also a good transition medium from what the baby has been fed by its mother and the formula it will be given.

Use fluids several times the first hour, then begin to space feedings according to the size of the infant. A tiny baby will usually need to be fed every two hours, a larger baby every four hours. A rehabilitator will begin to introduce formula into the fluids, starting with a 1 part to 4 part mix for a few feedings, then 1 to 3, 1 to 2, and then finally all formula. If at any time there is diarrhea, it is necessary to go back to the previous mix and progress more slowly. Always feed baby mammals on their stomachs, never on their backs to prevent choking and aspiration (inhaling liquid into lungs produces a pneumonia-like condition).

You can get puppy milk replacer or kitten milk replacer from your veterinarian, pet store, or feed and grain store where animal supplies are sold. As a general rule, squirrels, rabbits, opossum, and woodchuck babies need puppy milk replacer, raccoons need kitten milk replacer.

Baby mammals with their eyes closed need to be stimulated to go to the bathroom after each meal (their mothers lick them in the wild to stimulate and clean). You can do this by gently rubbing the anal/genital area with a soft tissue or a piece of cotton moistened with warm water. Moving about on their blankets will sometimes stimulate the baby enough to release a little urine or stool, but not enough. Once the eyes are opened, this process can be eliminated.

Birds

Baby birds need a nest of some kind to support them. A berry box with scrunched tissues works well, or a ring of twisted paper towels the right size for your birds, with layers of tissues over it. The tissues right under the bird's feet should be scrunched, not smooth, so that the baby does not slip and sprawl. The tissues must be changed often to keep the nest clean.

Both nestlings and fledglings need to be fed a formula that provides the same food values that its parents provided. A temporary formula can be made from dry cat food or puppy chow soaked in warm water and cut into tiny bits. Baby birds need to be fed about every twenty to thirty minutes, with the time between feedings increasing as the birds gets older. Some birds will gape, some birds need help (gently!) in opening their beaks. You may use tip of finger for larger birds to insert food. For tiny birds, use a swab stick without the cotton. By the time the bird is trying to fly, the feedings will be two hours apart. Please read about the kinds of diet your bird requires in the wild, as the wrong nutrition (feeding grain to an insect-eating or worm-eating bird, for instance) will actually starve it. **Do not feed bread and water. Even in the wild, bread is false calories that make the bird feel full without any nutritional value.** (If you are prone to feed birds as you walk, carry cracked corn in your pocket.)

hatchling

*nestling
day 9*

*fledgling
day 13*

Ages & Stages of Birds
(Cedar Waxwing)

Get Help

As you can tell, caring for wild young requires training and information. You should get the babies to a trained and licensed rehabilitator who will know the details of this baby's care. If this is not immediately possible, you can find details to help you care for them temporarily in the books from the 6-volume "I Found a Baby" BASIC MANUAL WILDLIFE REHABILITATION SERIES by Dale Carlson, Bick Publishing House. (See order forms in the back of this book.)

Captive Housing

When deciding on housing, choose a cage or container that will make your job of caring for the animal easy. An animal with a wound that needs to be tended to often should be in a cage that allows you to reach the animal without having to chase it each time. An animal with injured legs or wings should be in a small cage or container so that movement is restricted, and the injured part allowed to heal. Make sure that there is nothing in the cage that the animal can hurt itself on. Wire cages are hard on a bird's feathers, especially if the bird is nervous and flutters

Natural captive housing

around each time you approach. **Do not underestimate the ability of wild creatures to escape.**

Wire cages such as a dog cage wrapped in hardware cloth are excellent but cover the wire bottom to protect feet and claws. Newspaper is cheap and absorbent (never use the color parts) and paper toweling can be used to keep the ink from touching the animal. Pine chips, hay, natural materials like soil and leaves are good if there are no open wounds. Pet carriers, plastic boxes with ventilation holes, cardboard boxes, plastic baskets, all these will do.

Wild mammal babies will be comforted by soft cloths to snuggle in and hide under.

Nest boxes are important. They provide comfort, security, and a needed place to hide. A smaller cardboard or wooden box, basket, plastic box will do.

If your animal is older and closer to being ready to be released, the cage should more closely resemble the natural habitat, with branches, leaves, logs, and rocks.

CAPTIVE JUVENILE AND ADULT DIET

Read to find out the natural diet of the adult in the wild and provide an appropriate substitute diet. Poor nutrition will delay healing. Size and shape of the feeding dishes must conform to the needs of the animals. Dog and cat food can always be used as a staple.

Fresh water must be available at all times. Make sure that the water container is the right size and shape for the animal. A tiny bird will have trouble drinking from a large bowl of water. Water bottles fixed to the sides of cages for mammals need to be at the correct height for the mammal to drink comfortably.

Release a rabbit

RELEASE

Often your emergency first aid will be sufficient to make the animal ready for release. It must be healthy and able to care for itself in the wild. If it is possible and safe, the release site will be the place where you rescued it. The animal is familiar with the place and knows where to find food and water, even its parents or children.

Often the rescue site will not be a safe place and to release the animal there would put it back into a dangerous situation. In that case, choose a new site that has a food supply, water source, and the same species. This will ensure appropriate habitat. Make certain the new site is not too near human habitats, roads, and hunting sites, and is not already too crowded with wildlife. Never release an animal into a tree or hole in the ground. It may be home to a wild critter already.

Make certain of a three-day good weather forecast. Leave a supply of food for at least the first feeding.

6
EUTHANASIA: KINDNESS

Sometimes an animal is so seriously ill or injured that rehabilitation is impossible. Sometimes we are able to save an animal's life but the quality of that life is too sad, painful, unacceptable.

The decision to euthanize an animal ought to be made as objectively as possible. This is easy to do when the illnesses or injuries are devastating. When there is no hope for recovery, the choice is clear. When there is doubt, the decision can be very difficult. Each case will be unique. How to make the decision will be based on an estimation of all the elements of the animal's current health and future prognosis. It will be based on the animal's pain, its ability to survive in its now limited condition, its personal courage, your personal empathy, whether you can do a soft release and keep watch over it, whether it must be released back into the wild on its own. The decision must also be based on your time and workload, the quality of life for the animal, the long-term prognosis, the presence of disease dangerous to its own or other species, including humans, and again, its own level of pain.

It is best not to make the decision alone. Consult with others who are involved with animals, wildlife rehabilitators, your veterinarian. Be part of a group or a network; be affiliated with a rehabilitation center.

Take your time with this decision. Euthanasia cannot be reversed.

Animals that could not survive in the wild without pain and difficulty should be set free with the kindness of euthanasia.

Here are some typical situations where there is no hope for a good life for the animal.

- an animal that cannot feed or care for itself, or is so weak as to be easy prey for predators
- a mammal that has lost two or more legs
- any animal with a break in the spinal cord
- an animal with no bottom jaw
- an animal paralyzed with no sign of improvement after a week of treatment
- any animal suspected of a disease contagious to humans, like leptospirosis and rabies

The goal of euthanasia is to provide a good death, and to end the animal's suffering in the quickest and kindest way possible. **This means to render the animal unconscious before death occurs.**

There are both mechanical and chemical ways to euthanize that are acceptable.

MECHANICAL WAYS

- Gunshot. This requires training to be done so that people and other animals are not endangered and the animal does not suffer. The shot must be directly into the animal's brain.

- Suffocation causes terror, misery, and pain for the animal and is **not** acceptable.

CHEMICAL MEANS: INJECTIONS

Almost always in all states, only veterinarians or licensed personnel are allowed to inject. But injections with any of several death-causing agents are the most kind, efficient, effective method of euthanasia.

Phenobarbital or a mixture of barbiturates and cardiac toxins can be administered. But remember: These and all human medicines require a license to acquire or administer, and must be administered by a veterinarian.

The animal remains are not fit as food when these agents are used and cannot go back into the food chain.

CHEMICAL MEANS: INHALANTS

- Ether. This is effective but explosive. It is obtainable in the form of automobile starter fluid. Rehabilitators who use this put themselves at risk of setting themselves on fire, causing explosions, or endangering their own respiratory states by inhaling some of the fumes. There is also some suffering on the part of the animal.

- CO (carbon monoxide). This is not recommended. It is usually administered via car exhaust, but the animal suffers from the gas by-products, the heat and irritants, before death.

- CO_2 (carbon dioxide). This is the best of the inhalants. It meets the standards for painless death because it renders the animal unconscious rapidly, before respiratory arrest occurs. The American Veterinary Medical Association says this occurs within 6 minutes.

   A carbon dioxide chamber does not require extensive training to use properly. A tank of compressed carbon dioxide is connected to the appropriate size container with proper hardware fittings, and the animal placed gently within. CO_2 is very minimally hazardous to us, it is not flammable or explosive, and does not contaminate the animal who can then be buried shallowly and be returned to the food chain.

If this is the method of choice—and you acquire your license as a wildlife rehabilitator—you can contact the International Wildlife Rehabilitation Association, a veterinarian, or a rehabilitator or center for instructions on how to construct a chamber.

Larger Animals

To deal with larger animals, you may ask your local conservation officer to come and kill the animal by shooting it. You may also be able to take the larger animal to the local animal control facility and ask the animal control officer to euthanize it. Check first on the kindness of procedures before you do this.

Now that the choice has been made and carried through in the best way possible, you must begin to deal with your emotions.

Comfort yourself by knowing that you cared enough to help, and that your animal died warm, fed, and safe from fear and predators. James Herriot said on euthanasia in *All Things Wise and Wonderful,* "I hated doing this, painless though it was, but to me there has always been a comfort in the knowledge that the last thing these helpless animals knew was the sound of a friendly voice and the touch of a gentle hand."

7
GRIEF

In the process of caring for wild animals, there are occasions for great happiness, and there are also occasions for sadness and grief.

Grieving is an emotion we experience from a loss. An animal in your care may die and you will feel grief and recognize it as such. Euthanasia, even necessary and done painlessly and efficiently, may cause you to feel grief.

An animal that has done well in your care and has been released may cause you to feel a strong sense of loss. You worry about what will happen to the animal out there without your care. And you miss it.

When you hear of cruelty to animals, and neglect, you feel strong emotions of sadness, anger, and frustration. This is grief. It can combine anger, fear of death, feelings of vulnerability, a sense of loss.

Society does not offer much sympathy to a person grieving about an animal. Your grief is genuine, valid, and painful.

Acknowledge your grief. Talk it over with someone who will understand. Don't let it discourage you, or become self pity or utter tiredness. Accept grief as well as the joy of rescue, and then move on. The wild things need you. They need you to be there ready to help them with the next emergency.

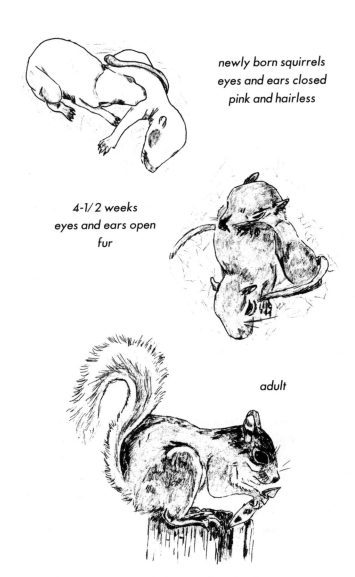

newly born squirrels
eyes and ears closed
pink and hairless

4-1/2 weeks
eyes and ears open
fur

adult

Ages & Stages of Squirrels

8
MAKE LIFE EASIER FOR WILDLIFE

There are simple things that we humans can do to reduce the casualties, and to make life easier for wildlife.

Plant shrubbery around the edge of your property to give wild animals a place to hide, and to live. These plants could be berry bushes planted just for the wild creatures.

Consider letting part of your yard go wild, leaving logs, brush piles, allowing bramble, vines, undergrowth to flourish as shelter for them.

Put out water for wildlife in all seasons.

If you have free roaming cats, and want to feed birds, make sure that the feeders hang free and are not near bushes where the cats can hide to sneak up on the birds. If you have free roaming cats, seriously consider not feeding birds, or keeping the cats inside. Vets say that people whose cats are outdoors even part of the time spend over twice as much on the care of their cats as people whose cats are indoors. Outdoor cats are victims of car hits, fights with other animals, cuts and scrapes, punctures, poisoning, and parasites. A large percentage of the small birds and mammals brought to rehabilitators are cat caught. Cat saliva has a bacteria in it that is devastating to a small critter and will cause infection and eventually death within 72 hours. Most cats, even those that have spent all of their lives outdoors, can adapt quite well to a life indoors. At the very least, **double-bell** your outdoor cat to give the other critters a chance.

Caps installed on chimneys will keep mammals and birds from nesting in them or coming in out of the cold. Keeping any holes in attics, windows in basements repaired and covered will prevent wildlife from coming in to nest or get warm or find food.

Do not feed your pets outdoors if you don't want to feed wildlife as well. They WILL find the food, they WILL come back for more.

Keep your fences in good repair. Exposed nails, loose wires, and holes in fences are all dangerous to the animals roaming in your area.

Obey road speed limits. Sometimes, go even slower. If there is an area where animals frequently cross, or if the roads are slicker than usual, then reduce your speed even more. Be able to stop or turn to avoid a collision without putting yourself in danger.

When you spot road kill, with your shovel or wearing gloves move it to the side of the road to keep predators from becoming the next victim while feeding.

Secure your trash. Creatures like raccoons are hungry enough and clever enough to eat what they can find.

Be alert for signs of movement on the side of the road when you are driving, and be ready to stop if an animal darts out. At night, watch for pairs of eyes shining with reflected headlights.

Perhaps the most important thing you can do is share with other people your information about animals and animal behavior. Share particularly that animals feel fear and pain, and pleasure and love for their young, just as we do. Advocate for them. The more people understand animals, the more they will show love, respect, and compassion for them.

APPENDIX
REFERENCE BOOKS

Audubon Handbooks, McGraw-Hill Book Company, New York, San Francisco, Singapore, Toronto, et al.

The Merck Veterinary Manual, Merck & Co., Inc., Rahway, New Jersey.

Peterson Field Guide Series, A Field Guide to the Mammals of North America, North of Mexico, A Field Guide to Birds (regional), by Roger Tory Peterson, Houghton, Mifflin Company, Boston.

Stokes Nature Guides, A Guide to Animal Tracking and Behavior, A Guide to Bird Behavior, Volume I, II, III, by Donald Stokes, Little, Brown and Company, Boston.

RECOMMENDED MANUALS

Basic Manual Wildlife Rehabilitation Series (7-VOL), Bick Publishing House, Madison, Connecticut. 203/245-0073.

Basic Wildlife Rehabilitation, 1AB, International Wildlife Rehabilitation Council, Suisun, California. 707/864-1761.

Introduction to Wildlife Rehabilitation, National Wildlife Rehabilitators Association, Carpenter Nature Center, Hastings, Minnesota. 651/690-3077.

Wild Animal Care and Rehabilitation, The Kalamazoo Nature Center, Kalamazoo, Michigan. 616/381-1574.

Wildlife Care and Rehabilitation, Brukner Nature Center, Troy, Ohio. 937/698-6493

Wildlife Rescue, Inc, Austin, Texas.512/472-9453

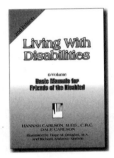